FRENCH
FOR BEGINNERS
PUZZLE WORKBOOK
Shopping and Eating

Rachel Bladon

Illustrated by John Shackell

Designed by Diane Thistlethwaite

Language consultant: Brigitte Montagne

Series editor: Nicole Irving

CONTENTS

la cassette **la glace** **le livre** **le bonbon** **la bande dessinée** **la pomme** **le crayon** **le chocolat**

Shopping

In this book, all the French words you will need to do the puzzles are shown in the Word checks and the pictures. There are also some words on page 1. You can find answers to all the puzzles on pages 28 to 30.

The puzzles on these two pages will help you say hello and goodbye to people when you are shopping. They also practise some useful French words for things.

Word check

bonjour	hello, good morning /afternoon
bonsoir	good evening
au revoir	goodbye

When talking to an adult you don't know well, it is polite to add the French for "Mr." (**Monsieur**) or "Mrs." (**Madame**) to your greeting, even if you don't know the person's name. For example, **Bonjour, Madame** is a polite way to say hello to a woman.

merci	thank you
voilà	there you are, there you go
pardon	sorry

Words for things

Words for things (called "nouns") are all either "masculine" or "feminine" in French.

The word for "the" is **le** before masculine nouns and **la** before feminine ones, but before nouns that begin with "a", "e", "i", "o" or "u" (and often "h"), it is **l'**. Whenever you learn the word for a thing in French, always try to learn it with the right word for "the".

le timbre	stamp
la pêche	peach
le croissant	croissant
la bague	ring

In word lists, [m] or [f] after a **l'** noun tells you if it is masculine or feminine:

l'abricot [m]	apricot
l'écharpe [f]	scarf

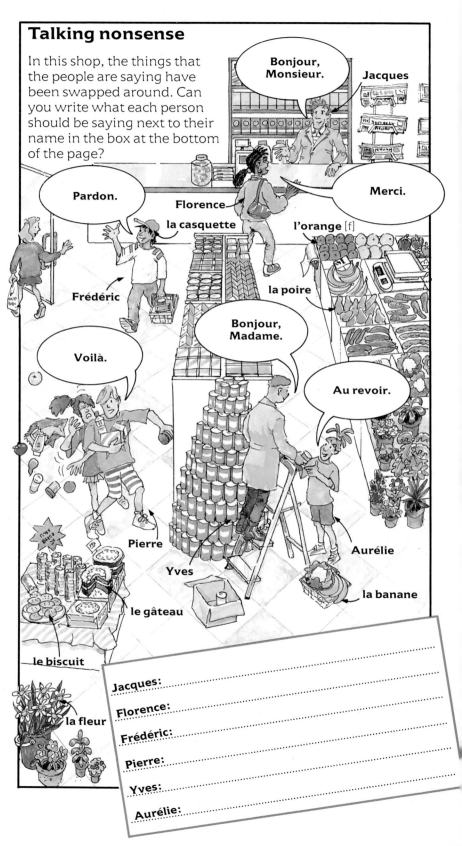

Talking nonsense

In this shop, the things that the people are saying have been swapped around. Can you write what each person should be saying next to their name in the box at the bottom of the page?

Bonjour, Monsieur.

Jacques

Pardon.

Florence

la casquette

Merci.

l'orange [f]

Frédéric

la poire

Bonjour, Madame.

Voilà.

Au revoir.

Aurélie

Pierre

Yves

la banane

le gâteau

le biscuit

la fleur

Jacques:

Florence:

Frédéric:

Pierre:

Yves:

Aurélie:

Word search

The French names of nine things are hidden in this grid without **le**, **la** or **l'**. Can you find them and write them out with the correct words for "the"? Use one list for **le** words, one for **la** words and another for **l'** words. (Remember, all the words you will need are shown on these two pages or on page 1.)

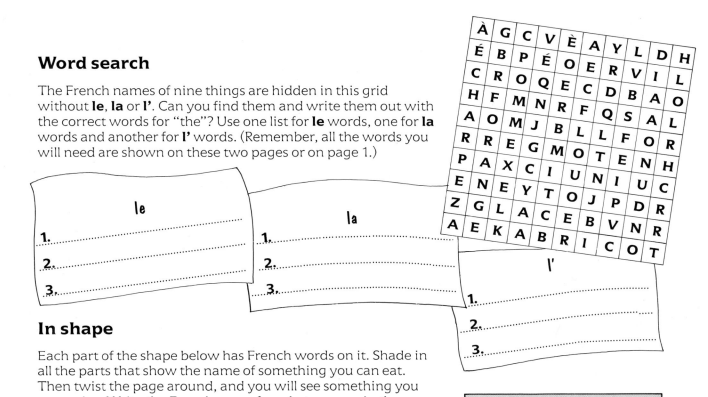

À	G	C	V	È	A	Y	L	D	H
É	B	P	É	O	E	R	V	I	L
C	R	O	Q	E	C	D	B	A	O
H	F	M	N	R	F	Q	S	A	L
A	O	M	J	B	L	L	F	O	R
R	R	E	G	M	O	T	E	N	H
P	A	X	C	I	U	N	I	U	C
E	N	E	Y	T	O	J	P	D	R
Z	G	L	A	C	E	B	V	N	R
A	E	K	A	B	R	I	C	O	T

le

1. ....
2. ....
3. ....

la

1. ....
2. ....
3. ....

l'

1. ....
2. ....
3. ....

In shape

Each part of the shape below has French words on it. Shade in all the parts that show the name of something you can eat. Then twist the page around, and you will see something you recognize. Write the French name for what you see in the grey space. (Don't forget **le**, **la** or **l'**.)

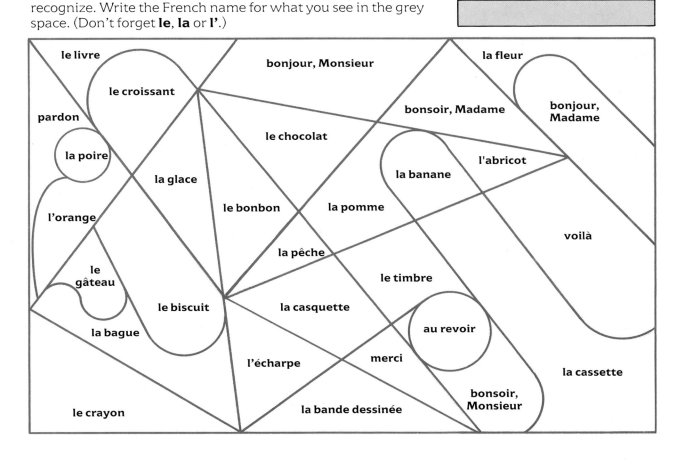

le livre
le croissant
bonjour, Monsieur
la fleur
pardon
bonsoir, Madame
bonjour, Madame
la poire
le chocolat
la glace
l'abricot
la banane
l'orange
le bonbon
la pomme
le gâteau
la pêche
voilà
le biscuit
le timbre
la casquette
la bague
au revoir
l'écharpe
merci
la cassette
le crayon
la bande dessinée
bonsoir, Monsieur

3

Shopping around

Here are some puzzles which use lots of the French words you need for buying things. They also give you practice of shop names.

Word check

le magasin	shop, store
la pharmacie	chemist's, pharmacy
la boulangerie	baker's
la boucherie	butcher's
le marchand de fruits et légumes	fruit and vegetable shop/stall
la pâtisserie	cake shop
le supermarché, le libre-service	supermarket
l'hypermarché* [m]	hypermarket, large supermarket
le traiteur, la charcuterie	delicatessen
la confiserie	sweet shop

In France you will also find a shop called **le bureau de tabac** (tobacconist). This is like a newsagent's, and usually sells newspapers, stamps, sweets and postcards.

"A" or "an" is **un** before masculine words and **une** before feminine ones. **Un** and **une** are also the words for "one".

un petit pain	a bread roll
un ballon	a ball
une carte postale	a postcard
une brosse à dents	a toothbrush
je voudrais	I would like
s'il vous plaît	please
oui	yes
non	no
c'est combien?	how much is it/that?
ça fait combien?	how much does that come to?

French money: there are 100 **centimes** in **un franc**.

un franc	one franc
deux francs	two francs

On shop signs, you will often see **franc** written as **F**, for example, **2F** means **deux francs**.

Shopping in Chèreville

Danielle has drawn pictures of the six things she wants to buy. She gets them all in the order shown on her list, buying one thing from each shop in Chèreville. Can you mark Danielle's route on the town plan? (She never goes along the same part of a street twice.)

Write six sentences in the blue boxes to show how Danielle asks for the things on her list. (Begin each one with **Je voudrais un** or **Je voudrais une**...)

1.
2.
3.

Cartoon confusion

Two separate cartoon stories, each made up of six pictures, have been jumbled up (below and on the right). The first picture of one story is marked "1", and the first picture of the other story is marked "A". Decide which pictures make up which story. Then mark them in order, from 2 to 6 and B to F.

* Remember, you often use **l'** with words that begin with "h".

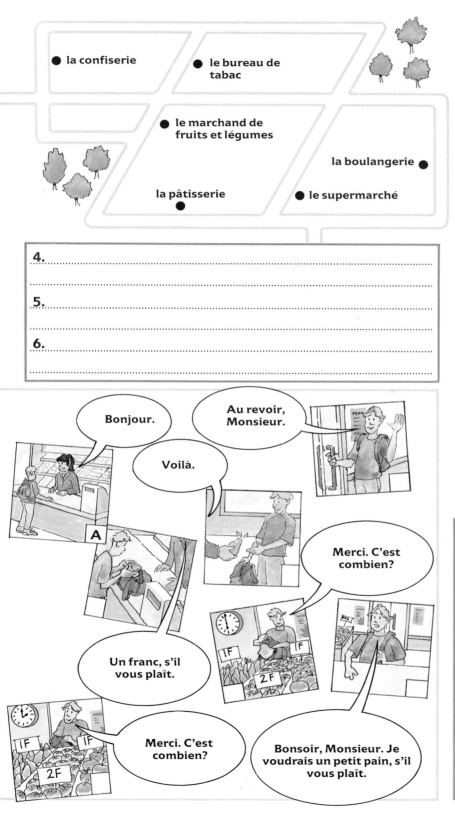

la confiserie

le bureau de tabac

le marchand de fruits et légumes

la boulangerie

la pâtisserie

le supermarché

4. ....

5. ....

6. ....

Bonjour.

Au revoir, Monsieur.

Voilà.

A

Merci. C'est combien?

Un franc, s'il vous plaît.

Merci. C'est combien?

Bonsoir, Monsieur. Je voudrais un petit pain, s'il vous plaît.

Word chain

In this grid, the French names for the twelve things listed below are arranged in a chain (without words for "the"). To find them, start from the middle letter "G" and move up, down, left or right by one or more letters. Then, in the blue box, write out the words you have found. (Keep to the order of the word chain and add **le**, **la** or **l'**.)

banana   biscuit
book   butcher's
cap   cassette
croissant   ice-cream
peach   pear
scarf   stamp

R	E	C	A	T	N	A	S	S
V	I	L	S	S	E	T	T	I
T	I	E	I	R	E	H	E	O
E	M	B	B	O	U	C	C	R
P	R	R	E	G	B	I	S	C
H	A	T	T	L	E	T	I	U
C	É	E	E	A	C	P	Ê	C
A	S	Q	U	A	B	I	O	H
C	E	N	A	N	E	R	P	E

1. ....
2. ....
3. ....
4. ....
5. ....
6. ....
7. ....
8. ....
9. ....
10. ....
11. ....
12. ....

At the market

These puzzles are all about buying things from the market and counting up to twenty.

Word check

Here is the French action word, or verb, **avoir** (to have, to have got). Like all verbs, it changes (has slightly different words) when different people do the action:

j'ai	I have (got)
tu as	you have (got)
il/elle a	he/she has (got)
nous avons	we have (got)
vous avez	you have (got)
ils/elles ont	they have (got)

The French for "I", **je**, turns into **j'** before words that begin with "a", "e", "i", "o" and "u".

Notice that French has two words for "you", **tu** and **vous**. **Tu** is what you say to a friend, a relative or someone your own age. You use **vous** for an adult you don't know well, and for more than one person.

tu as?, vous avez?	do you have?
le marché	market
le marchand de fromages	cheese stall
c'est	it/that is
ça fait	that comes to
et	and
la pomme de terre	potato
la tomate	tomato
la baguette	French stick
le sac en plastique	plastic bag

Numbers 1-20

1	**un, une**	11	**onze**
2	**deux**	12	**douze**
3	**trois**	13	**treize**
4	**quatre**	14	**quatorze**
5	**cinq**	15	**quinze**
6	**six**	16	**seize**
7	**sept**	17	**dix-sept**
8	**huit**	18	**dix-huit**
9	**neuf**	19	**dix-neuf**
10	**dix**	20	**vingt**

"One" is **un** before masculine words and **une** before feminine words.*

When you are talking about more than one thing, you add "s" to the end of most French nouns, and the word for "the" is always **les**:

la saucisse	sausage
les saucisses	sausages

Market mix-up

While Katie is on holiday in France, she goes to the market to buy food for a picnic with her pen pal. Decide what everyone would say in these situations, and put A, B or C in each speech bubble to show which is the right piece of French.

1. At the fruit and vegetable stall, Katie greets the woman who is serving:

A. **Bonjour, Madame.**
B. **Bonjour, Monsieur.**
C. **Au revoir, Madame.**

2. She asks for some fruit for the picnic:

A. **Je voudrais une pomme de terre et deux oranges, s'il vous plaît.**
B. **Je voudrais un ballon et une pomme, s'il vous plaît.**
C. **Je voudrais deux bananes et une poire, s'il vous plaît.**

3. Bananas are two francs each, and pears are one franc. When Katie asks how much she has to pay, she is told:

A. **Ça fait trois francs.**
B. **Ça fait cinq francs.**
C. **Ça fait quatre francs.**

4. When she has paid, she asks:

A. **Tu as un sac en plastique?**
B. **Vous avez une bague?**
C. **Vous avez un sac en plastique, s'il vous plaît?**

5. The woman hands her a bag and replies:

A. **Non.**
B. **Oui. Voilà.**
C. **Oui, merci.**

6. Katie stops at the cheese stall, where she spends eleven francs, and then goes to the baker's. She asks for a French stick, and the man serving says:

A. **Une baguette? C'est quatre francs.**
B. **Une saucisse? C'est sept francs.**
C. **Deux baguettes? Ça fait huit francs.**

7. At lunchtime, Katie looks for the food she has bought. Oh no! She has left everything at the baker's. Her pen pal asks her how much money she has wasted, and she groans:

A. **Neuf francs.**
B. **Vingt francs.**
C. **Dix-huit francs.**

---

* Remember, **un** and **une** also mean "a" (or "an").

Big spenders

Find what these children are saying in the box below and fill in their speech bubbles. (You will not need everything in the box.)

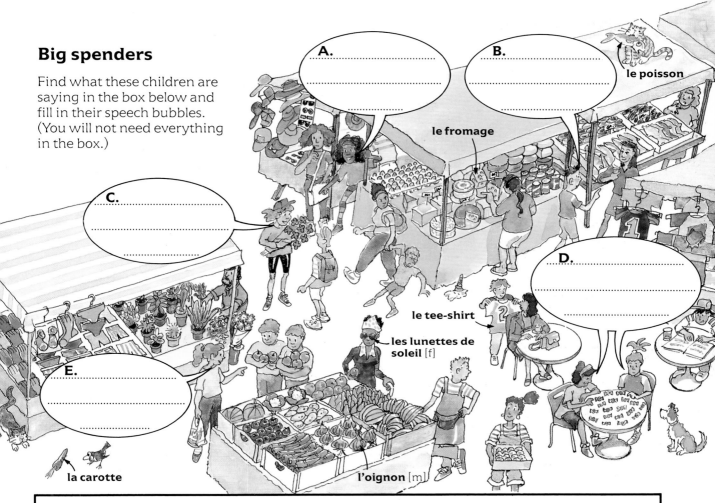

A. ....

B. ....

le poisson

le fromage

C. ....

D. ....

le tee-shirt

les lunettes de soleil [f]

E. ....

la carotte

l'oignon [m]

J'ai neuf fleurs.	Nous avons dix-sept bonbons.	Elle a une casquette.
Tu as une glace.	J'ai huit fleurs.	Nous avons dix-huit bonbons.
Il a une casquette.	Tu as sept pommes.	Vous avez sept pommes.

Clued-up

Use the clues below to write out the correct numbers in French across the grid. Your answers will spell another number down the grey column. Then look at the sums A, B, C, D and E (on the right), and circle the one that gives you this number.

1. Toes on one foot.
2. Months in a year.
3. Quarters in a whole.
4. Legs on a spider.
5. Players in a soccer team.
6. Legs on a tripod.
7. Unlucky for some.
8. Wonders of the world.

A. **Vingt – quatre.**
B. **Six + sept.**
C. **Neuf + six.**
D. **Dix-neuf – cinq.**
E. **Cinq + huit.**

At the hypermarket

These puzzles use lots of the French you need for shopping in "hypermarkets" (large supermarkets you will often come across in France).

Word check

l'entrée [f]	entrance
la sortie	exit
ouvert	open
fermé	closed
le caddie	trolley
le panier	basket
les vêtements [m]	clothes
l'équipement sportif [m]	sports gear
le pain	bread
la viande	meat
le jambon	ham
les chips [f]	crisps
l'eau [f]	water

un paquet de	a packet of
un morceau de	a piece of
une tranche de	a slice of
un kilo de	a kilo of
cent grammes de	a hundred grammes of

The five pieces of French above all end in **de** (of) and are used with the name of a thing (such as **le jambon**). After them, though, you must drop **le**, **la** or **l'** from the name, for example, "a slice of ham" is **une tranche de jambon**. If the name begins with "a", "e", "i", "o" or "u", **de** turns into **d'**.

encore un peu	a little more
un peu moins	a little less
où est?	where is?
où sont?	where are?
ce fromage	this cheese
c'est tout?	is that all?
là-bas	over there
près de	near
avec	with
comme ça?	like that?

French has different words for "some", depending on whether you are talking about a **le**, **la**, **l'** or **les** word. For **la** and **l'** words, you put **de** in front:

de la viande	some meat
de l'eau	some water

For **le** and **les** words, you drop **le** and **les** and use **du** and **des**:

du chocolat	some chocolate
des bonbons	some sweets

Torn in two

Pair off the pieces of French in these blue labels to find six sentences. Then look at the pictures below. Can you match each of the sentences with a speech bubble to make six little conversations? Fill in the spaces 1 to 6 with the right sentences.

Oui, s'il vous plaît. Et un morceau

l'équipement sportif, s'il vous plaît?

vingt francs.   Où est

les vêtements, s'il vous plaît?

un peu, s'il vous plaît.

Un kilo de   Où sont

pommes, s'il vous plaît.

de ce fromage.

Ça fait   Encore

1.
....
....
....

C'est tout?

Ça fait combien?

2.
....
....

Comme ça?

Deux tranches de jambon?

3.
....
....
....

4.
....
....
....

5.
....
....
....

6.
....
....
....

Là-bas, près de l'entrée.

Là-bas, avec les vêtements.

Twin shoppers

Nathalie and Frédéric have each bought three things that the other did not get. Can you write three sentences to say which things only Nathalie has, and three to say which ones only Frédéric has? Begin your answers with the French for "She has ..." or "He has ...", and use the right words for "a" or "some".

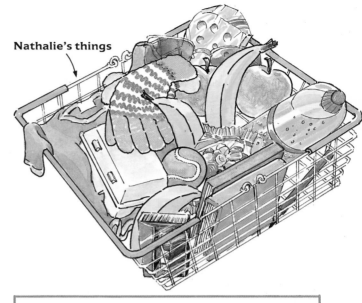

Nathalie's things

Frédéric's things

1.	
2.	
3.	
4.	
5.	
6.	

Shopping search

Hidden in this grid are the French names for the nine things that Céline wants to buy. Can you find them and write sentences for her to say what she wants? Begin your answers with **Je voudrais** and use the right words for "some" or "a".

A	T	R	I	H	S	E	E	T
B	L	Y	H	A	O	G	B	C
I	D	F	P	M	L	F	D	A
S	G	T	I	A	C	O	V	S
C	H	I	C	H	I	P	S	S
U	N	E	C	A	R	N	K	E
I	X	N	O	B	M	A	J	T
T	P	O	I	R	E	S	W	T
S	A	V	J	L	I	V	R	E

1.	
2.	
3.	
4.	
5.	
6.	
7.	
8.	
9.	

Other shops in town

The puzzles on these two pages use shop names and lots of numbers.

Word check

la librairie	bookshop
le magasin de photo	camera shop
la papeterie	stationer's
le magasin de musique	music shop
le magasin de sport	sports shop
le magasin de vêtements	clothes shop
la bibliothèque	library
l'agence de voyages [f]	travel agent's
l'office du tourisme* [m]	tourist office

la rue	street
l'arbre [m]	tree
la pellicule	(camera) film
la trousse	pencil case
le cahier	exercise book
la règle	ruler
l'autocollant [m]	sticker
est	is

derrière	behind
devant	in front of
entre	between
en face de	opposite
à côté de	next to
au bout de	at the end of

When you use **en face de**, **à côté de** and **au bout de** in front of **le** or **les** words, **de** turns into **du** or **des** (and you drop **le** and **les**):

en face du magasin	opposite the shop
à côté des magasins	next to the shops

With **la** and **l'** words, **de** just goes in front of **la** and **l'**:

au bout de la rue	at the end of the street
à côté de l'arbre	next to the tree

When you are talking about a mixture of francs and centimes, you don't use the word **centimes**. For example, **un franc vingt** is what you say for "one franc twenty (centimes)"

deux francs (pièce)	two francs (each)

Numbers 21-100

21	**vingt et un**	32	**trente-deux**	72	**soixante-douze**
22	**vingt-deux**	33	**trente-trois**	80	**quatre-vingts**
23	**vingt-trois**	40	**quarante**	81	**quatre-vingt-un**
24	**vingt-quatre**	50	**cinquante**	82	**quatre-vingt-deux**
25	**vingt-cinq**	60	**soixante**	90	**quatre-vingt-dix**
30	**trente**	70	**soixante-dix**	91	**quatre-vingt-onze**
31	**trente et un**	71	**soixante et onze**	100	**cent**

Bargain hunter

Pierre wants to get all the things shown here from one hypermarket, but he can't decide whether it will be cheaper to go to **Hypersoldes** or **Prix Cassés**.

Look at the pricelists and decide where he should go. Then add up what he will spend if he goes there, and what he will save. Write down (in French) the name of the hypermarket and both these amounts.

Hypersoldes	
un cahier	sept francs cinquante
une règle	neuf francs soixante-dix
un crayon	deux francs
une pellicule	quarante et un francs
une cassette	quatre-vingt-cinq francs
une carte postale	un franc cinquante
une brosse à dents	seize francs vingt
un kilo de poires	onze francs (deux francs pièce)
un kilo de bananes	huit francs
cent grammes de bonbons	quatre francs
un paquet de chips	onze francs quarante

Prix Cassés	
un kilo de poires	dix francs (un franc cinquante pièce)
un paquet de chips	dix francs soixante
une carte postale	un franc
une bande dessinée	huit francs
une pellicule	quarante et un francs
une cassette	quatre-vingt-onze francs
une brosse à dents	douze francs trente
un cahier	huit francs dix
une trousse	trente-deux francs
un crayon	trois francs
une règle	onze francs

The hypermarket Pierre should go to is: ....

He will spend: ....

He will save: ....

* Other words for "tourist office" are **la maison du tourisme** and **le syndicat d'initiative**.

Treasure trail

This list shows seven of the eight things you have to collect here, and the order you must collect them in. Find the animal that has the first thing, and it will tell you where to go next. Now decide how the rest of the animals should direct you to the other pieces of "treasure". Fill in their speech bubbles, beginning **à côté de**, **devant** or **en face de**. The last animal you come to will tell you where the eighth thing is. Write the French for this at the bottom of the list.

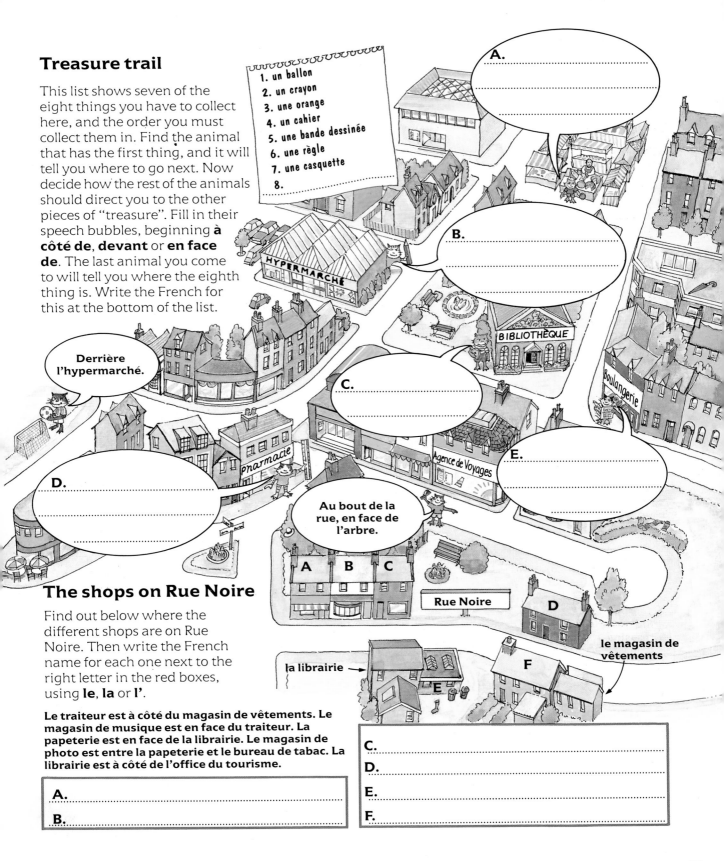

1. un ballon
2. un crayon
3. une orange
4. un cahier
5. une bande dessinée
6. une règle
7. une casquette
8.

A.

B.

C.

D.

E.

Derrière l'hypermarché.

Au bout de la rue, en face de l'arbre.

HYPERMARCHÉ

BIBLIOTHÈQUE

Boulangerie

pharmacie

Agence de Voyages

Rue Noire

A B C

D

E

F

la librairie

le magasin de vêtements

The shops on Rue Noire

Find out below where the different shops are on Rue Noire. Then write the French name for each one next to the right letter in the red boxes, using **le**, **la** or **l'**.

Le traiteur est à côté du magasin de vêtements. Le magasin de musique est en face du traiteur. La papeterie est en face de la librairie. Le magasin de photo est entre la papeterie et le bureau de tabac. La librairie est à côté de l'office du tourisme.

A.

B.

C.

D.

E.

F.

Getting around town

The puzzles on these two pages help you find the bank, buy stamps and use other services. They also give you some more number practice.

Word check

la poste	post office
la lettre	letter
la banque	bank
le bureau de change	foreign exchange desk/office
l'argent [m]	money
le traveller's chèque	traveller's cheque
changer	to change, to cash
le passeport	passport
la station-service	petrol station
l'essence [f]	petrol
le plein	a full tank (of petrol)
vérifier l'huile	to check the oil
la laverie automatique	launderette
la lessive	washing powder
la cabine téléphonique	phone booth
excusez-moi	excuse me
il y a un/une ... par ici?	is there a ... near here?
à gauche	on the left
à droite	on the right
vous pouvez (vérifier l'huile)?	can you (check the oil)?
votre (passeport)	your (passport)
aussi	also, as well
l'Angleterre [f]	England
pour	for, to
ou	or
le gobelet	cup, beaker
seulement	only

Going dotty

Join all the red dots from twenty to thirty, forty to fifty, sixty to seventy and eighty to ninety to make a maze. Then mark the route Claudine must take through it to find her dog.

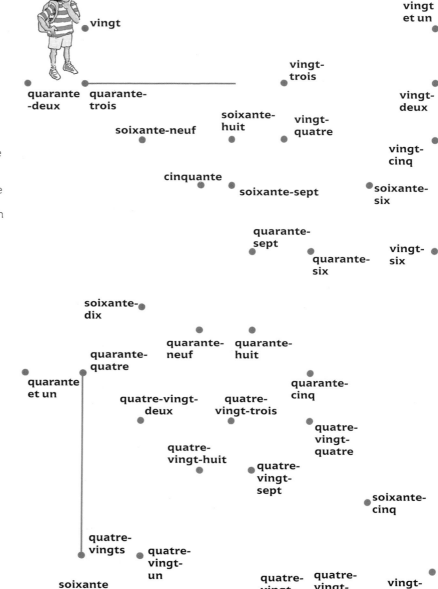

vingt

vingt et un

vingt-trois

vingt-deux

quarante-deux

quarante-trois

soixante-neuf

soixante-huit

vingt-quatre

vingt-cinq

vingt-six

soixante-six

cinquante

soixante-sept

quarante-sept

quarante-six

vingt-six

soixante-dix

quarante-neuf

quarante-huit

quarante-quatre

quarante et un

quarante-cinq

quatre-vingt-deux

quatre-vingt-trois

quatre-vingt-quatre

quatre-vingt-huit

quatre-vingt-sept

soixante-cinq

quatre-vingts

quatre-vingt-un

soixante et un

quatre-vingt-six

quatre-vingt-cinq

vingt-sept

soixante-deux

quatre-vingt-neuf

quatre-vingt-dix

soixante

quarante

soixante-trois

vingt-neuf

soixante-quatre

trente

vingt-neuf

vingt-huit

Picture matchmaking

Can you pair off the five pieces of French, A to E, with the numbered pieces, 1 to 5, to make five conversations? Match each of these with the correct picture and write the letter and number in the small boxes provided.

A. **Il y a une pharmacie par ici?**
B. **Vous avez de la lessive?**
C. **Le plein?**
D. **Un timbre pour l'Angleterre, s'il vous plaît.**
E. **Je voudrais changer un traveller's chèque, s'il vous plaît.**

1. **Oui. Et vous pouvez aussi vérifier l'huile, s'il vous plaît?**
2. **Pour une lettre ou une carte postale?**
3. **Vous avez votre passeport?**
4. **Oui, à gauche, en face de la poste.**
5. **Oui, c'est cinq francs pour un gobelet.**

Postcard palaver

First read this story about Louise and Martin trying to send a postcard home to Manchester. Then fill in the gaps in the numbered pieces of French (shown in heavier lettering). Write each piece out in the red box, adding the missing words.

Louise and Martin wanted a stamp for their postcard, so they stopped someone and asked: **1) "Excusez-moi. Où est ....?"** *When they got to the post office, Louise explained what she wanted:* **2) "Je voudrais ...., s'il vous plaît."** *Realizing they were English, the woman at the counter inquired* **3) "Pour ....?"** **4) "...., s'il vous plaît,"** *Louise nodded.* **5) "C'est ...."**, *said the woman, and Martin rummaged in his pocket for two francs twenty. Martin frowned, took out a franc and said:* **6) "J'ai seulement ...."**. *Louise and Martin apologized and asked:* **7) "Il y a .... par ici?"** **8) "Oui. À...., à côté .... ."** *the woman replied. They thanked her, said goodbye:* **9) "Merci.**

....", *and set off for the bank.*

Sure enough, Louise and Martin found the bank on the right, next to the bookshop. They asked a cashier where the foreign exchange desk was: **10) "Où est ....?"** *Louise explained what she wanted:* **11) "Je voudrais ...., s'il vous plaît."** *But the man at the desk shook his head - they did not cash traveller's cheques at that branch. He told Louise and Martin to take a bus to the bank at Pharville.*

An hour later, their pockets full of French francs, Louise and Martin returned to the post office. "Oh no!" cried Martin, pointing at the sign on the door, which read **12) "...."**. *"It's closed!"*

1.
....

....

2.
....

....

3.
....

4.
....

5.
....

6.
....

7.
....

8.
....

9.
....

10.
....

11.
....

....

12.
....

Opening hours

Here you can practise talking about the opening and closing times of shops and other useful places.

Telling the time

quelle heure est-il?	what time is it?
il est	it is
(il est) une heure	(it is) one o'clock
cinq heures	five o'clock
huit heures	eight o'clock
midi	midday, twelve o'clock

To say "past" the hour in French, you just say the hour and add the number of minutes:

huit heures cinq	five past eight

For "to", you say the hour and add **moins** (minus) and the number of minutes:

neuf heures moins dix	ten to nine
(quatre heures) et quart	quarter past (four)
(trois heures) et demie	half past (three)
(midi) moins le quart	quarter to (twelve)

Word check

When you are talking about a shop with a feminine name, such as **la boulangerie**, you add "e" to **ouvert** (open) and **fermé** (closed):

la boulangerie est ouverte	the baker's is open
la pharmacie est fermée	the chemist's is closed
à (six heures)	at (six o'clock)
de ... à	from ... until
de trois heures et demie à quatre heures et quart	from half past three until quarter past four
le matin	(in the) morning
le soir	(in the) evening

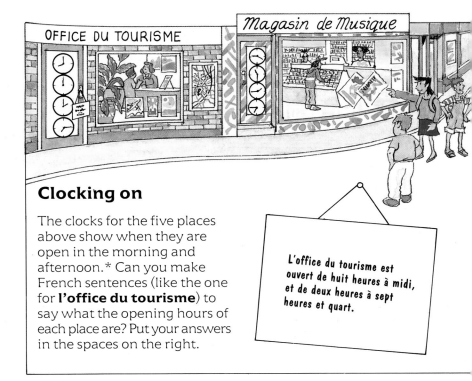

Clocking on

The clocks for the five places above show when they are open in the morning and afternoon.* Can you make French sentences (like the one for **l'office du tourisme**) to say what the opening hours of each place are? Put your answers in the spaces on the right.

L'office du tourisme est ouvert de huit heures à midi, et de deux heures à sept heures et quart.

Word circle

Look at the things numbered 1 to 6. For each one, think of a place where you might buy it. Then write the French name for this place around the word circle, without using words for "the". Its first letter must go in the space with the matching number, then one letter goes into each space until you reach the next number. (Three spaces already have letters in them.)

Now you will see something spelled out in the section shown by the arrow. Use the ten letters in grey spaces to spell the name for a shop where you might buy this. Write this shop name in the space below, adding the word for "the".

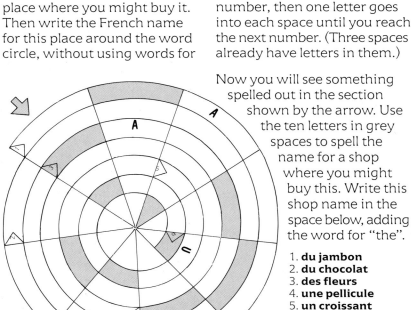

1. **du jambon**
2. **du chocolat**
3. **des fleurs**
4. **une pellicule**
5. **un croissant**
6. **un gâteau**

*In France, many shops and other places close for an hour or two at lunchtime.

1. ....
....

2. ....
....

3. ....

4. ....
....

Out of time

First read about the problems Flavien's friends are having with their watches (see right). Then fill in the speech bubbles to show how they all answer the waiter's question.

Frédéric's watch is ten minutes fast and Danielle's is running a quarter of an hour slower than his. Claudine's watch was fifteen minutes slow, but it stopped half an hour ago. Céline reset her watch by Claudine's an hour ago, and since then it has kept good time. Only Flavien's is showing the right time.

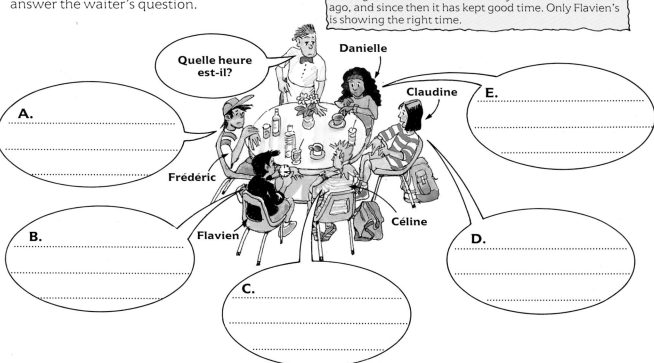

Mangetout Island

The puzzles on Mangetout Island will help you talk about things you like eating.

Word check

Here is the verb **aimer** (to like). Most verbs that end in "er" change in the same way as **aimer** when different people do the action.

j'aime	I like
tu aimes	you like
il/elle aime	he/she likes
nous aimons	we like
vous aimez	you like
ils/elles aiment	they like

For "it" in French, you use **il** to talk about a masculine word and **elle** to talk about a feminine one. For "they", you use **elles** for a feminine word. You use **ils** for a masculine word, and for masculine and feminine words together.

le petit déjeuner	breakfast
le déjeuner	lunch
le dîner	dinner (evening meal)
le pique-nique	picnic
j'ai faim	I'm hungry
j'ai soif	I'm thirsty
le beignet	doughnut
le pâté	pâté
les légumes [m]	vegetables
les petits-pois [m]	peas
les fruits [m]	fruit
la fraise	strawberry
les boissons [f]	drinks
le jus d'orange	orange juice
le café	coffee
le thé	tea

Which way?

Unscramble the words below to find the French names of eight things. Find these things on the island, then, for each one, write its name out on the blank sign that points along the road leading to it.

MOSSEETALT   QUIPLIE-QUEEN
SLONGOSINE   SISSEESCALUS
SPILCHES   BIGLEENTESS
COLTOLEACH   SLOANEGRUDJE

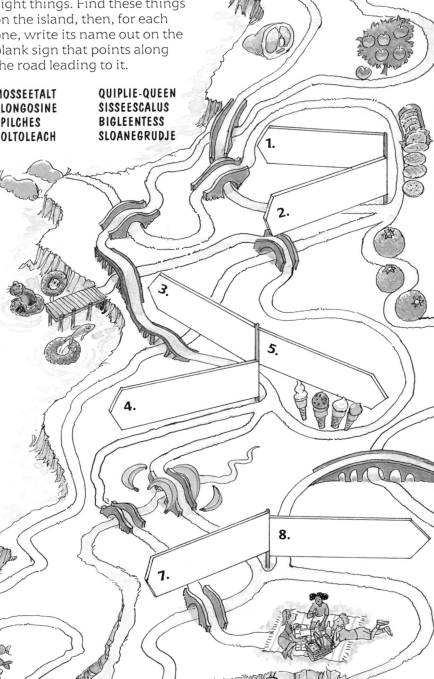

Mangetout Island

Triple treat

Below, Aurélie and her friends are all saying what their favourite thing is. Can you spot these things on the island, and then find the route each of them must take to get there? Along these routes, they will each find two other things they like. Write sentences below for all the characters shown, saying what these two things are. (Begin with the French for "He likes", "She likes", "It likes" or "They like".)

Nous aimons les beignets.

J'aime le chocolat.

J'aime les poires.

J'aime les saucisses.

Nous aimons les chips.

1. ....
2. ....
3. ....
4. ....
5. ....

Les Boissons
1. ....
2. ....
3. ....
4. ....

La Viande
1. ....
2. ....
3. ....

Les Légumes
1. ....
2. ....
3. ....
4. ....

6.

Les Fruits
1. ....
2. ....
3. ....
4. ....
5. ....
6. ....

Food sails

Look at the labels on these four ships' flags. Decide which of the things listed below go with which flag, and write them in the spaces on the correct sail. (There are five things on the list that you will not use.)

le café
le pâté
la glace
le jus d'orange
le petit pain
les petits-pois
la poire
le fromage
le thé
la banane
l'eau

la pomme
le bonbon
l'abricot
le gâteau
l'oignon
la pêche
le jambon
l'orange
la carotte
la saucisse
la pomme de terre

Likes and dislikes

Here you can get more practice of saying what food you like. These puzzles will also help you talk about the things you don't like eating.

Word check

manger	to eat
préférer	to prefer

Like most other verbs ending in "er", **manger** and **préférer** change in the same way as **aimer** (on page 16).*

les pâtes [f]	pasta (macaroni, noodles ...)
les spaghetti [m]	spaghetti
l'omelette [f]	omelette
le hamburger	hamburger
les frites [f]	chips
la pizza	pizza
le sandwich (au jambon)	(ham) sandwich
le sandwich (au fromage)	(cheese) sandwich
la salade	salad
le potage	soup
le lait	milk
l'oeuf [m]	egg
le yaourt	yoghurt
mais	but
je suis végétarien	I am a vegetarian (if you are a boy or man)
je suis végétarienne	I am a vegetarian (if you are a girl or woman)
le café	café
le restaurant	restaurant

In French, to say things like "I don't eat" or "I don't like", you put **ne** in front of the verb and **pas** after it:

je ne mange pas	I don't eat
tu ne manges pas	you don't eat

Ne turns into **n'** in front of words beginning with "a", "e", "i", "o" or "u":

je n'aime pas	I don't like
tu n'aimes pas	you don't like

Sentence splitters

Four sentences have been cut into four pieces and mixed up. The first piece of each one is written out in the box below. Can you fit the other pieces back together and write them in the correct spaces to complete each sentence?

> n'aiment pas le jus d'orange.
>
> aimez les
>
> nous aimons le yaourt.
>
> préfères la pizza.
>
> ils   aimes le
>
> aiment le lait mais
>
> n'aimons   pas les frites.
>
> spaghetti mais vous n'aimez
>
> potage mais tu
>
> pas les oeufs mais

1. **Vous** ....

2. **Ils** ....

3. **Tu** ....

4. **Nous** ....

The perfect picnic

Read what Céline and her friends are saying about what they especially like or dislike. Then look at the three picnic tables, A, B and C. Can you decide who should sit where, so that no one has anything they don't want on their table, and everyone has the thing they most like? Write two names on each table's list to show where everyone should sit.

On this picnic, there are two things that more than one person likes, and two things that more than one person doesn't like. Complete the four sentences in the orange sheet on the right to say what each pair of friends likes or dislikes.

> J'aime les chips. Je n'aime pas les tomates, et je n'aime pas le café.

> J'aime les sandwichs, mais je préfère les biscuits. Je suis végétarien.

Céline

Flavien

A. ....

....

---

* However, the second **é** of **préférer** changes to **è** for all except its **nous** and **vous** words, and **manger** has a slightly different **nous** word (**mangeons**).

French crossword

Use the clues to fill in the crossword. (Don't forget the different words for "a" or "the".)

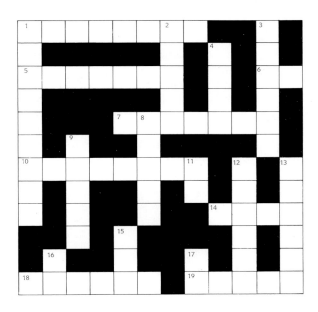

Across

1. Cauliflower is one. (2, 6)
5. What you say in French for "good morning". (7)
6. "Some" (with a masculine word). (2)
7. What you say when you are hungry. (1, 2, 4)
10. It might be red, green or yellow. (3, 5)
14. **Je mange une pizza** ... **de la salade.** (4)
18. **"... de bananes, s'il vous plaît."** (2, 4)
19. You can drink this on its own, or with milk or lemon. (2, 3)

Down

1. You might eat one with 19. (2, 7)
2. The French for "thank you". (5)
3. **"Bonjour, ..."** is how you greet a woman in a shop. (6)
4. "Some" (with a feminine word). (2, 2)
8. The French verb "to like". (5)
9. The French for "closed". (5)
11. The French for "and". (2)
12. The French for "open". (6)
13. For a meal, you go to **un restaurant**. For a drink or a snack, you go to ... . (2, 4)
15. "Some" (with a word that begins with "a", "e", "i", "o" or "u"). (2, 1)
16. "A" (with a masculine word). (2)
17. "It" (talking about a masculine thing). (2)

Mealtime talk

Here are some puzzles which use lots of the French you need when you get a meal ready or eat with other people.

Word check

la salle à manger	dining room
la cuisine	kitchen
le four	oven
l'évier [m]	sink
le frigo	fridge
la table	table
la chaise	chair
la poêle	frying pan
la casserole	saucepan
la farine	flour
le sucre	sugar

le sel	salt
les céréales [f]	cereals
la confiture	jam
faire la vaisselle	to do the washing up
à table	come to the table, it's ready
c'est bon?	is it good?
c'est délicieux	it's delicious
encore du/de la/ de l'/des...?*	some more...?
j'ai assez mangé	I've had enough (to eat)
dans	in
sous	under
sur	on
sont	are

je peux t'aider?	can I help you?
tu peux me passer (le beurre)?	can you pass me (the butter)?
sers-toi	help yourself
s'il te plaît	please

You only use the four expressions above when talking to a friend, a relative or someone your own age. For an adult you don't know well, or more than one person, you say:

je peux vous aider?	can I help you?
vous pouvez me passer...?	can you pass me...?
servez-vous	help yourself, help yourselves
s'il vous plaît	please

Hungry campers

Find what these children are saying in the panel on the side of the tent, and fill in each of their speech bubbles. (You will not need everything in the panel.)

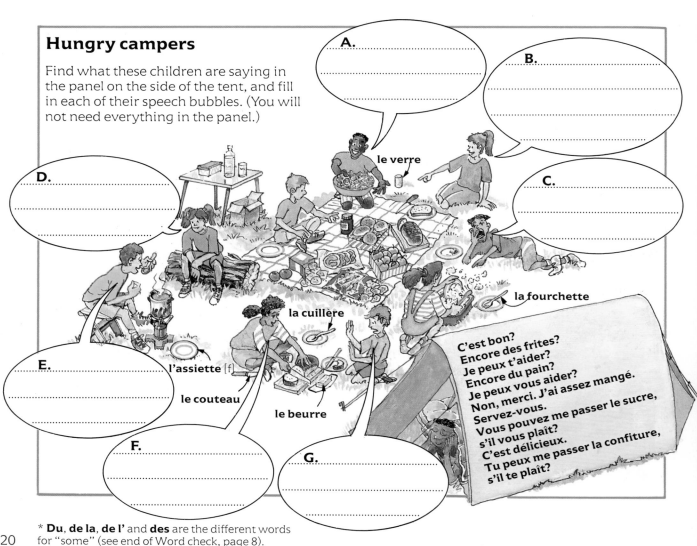

A.

B.

C.

D.

E.

F.

G.

le verre

la fourchette

la cuillère

l'assiette [f]

le couteau

le beurre

C'est bon?
Encore des frites?
Je peux t'aider?
Encore du pain?
Je peux vous aider?
Non, merci. J'ai assez mangé.
Servez-vous.
Vous pouvez me passer le sucre, s'il vous plaît?
C'est délicieux.
Tu peux me passer la confiture, s'il te plaît?

* **Du**, **de la**, **de l'** and **des** are the different words for "some" (see end of Word check, page 8).

Kitchen caper

Picture A below shows what the Champagne family kitchen looked like before Dominique started cooking. Picture B shows what it looks like afterwards. Decide which eight things Dominique has put away in the wrong place, then write French sentences to say where these things are now, using the words for "in", "on" or "under".

1.	**5.**
2.	**6.**
3.	**7.**
4.	**8.**

Word snake

Think of the French names for the things listed in the grey box. Write them along the word snake, putting the first letter of each one next to its number. Now fill the red grid with the circled letters to spell the name of something you can make with these things.

1. SOME CHEESE
2. SOME SALT
3. SOME BUTTER
4. SOME EGGS
5. SOME MILK
6. A FRYING PAN

									T

In the café

The puzzles on these two pages give you lots of practice of asking for things in cafés.

Word check

le café	(black) coffee
le (café) crème	white coffee
le thé	tea
au lait	with milk
au citron	with lemon
le chocolat (chaud)	hot chocolate
un verre de*	a glass of

le coca	coke
le jus de pomme	apple juice
le citron pressé	lemon drink
le croque-monsieur	cheese and ham on toast
vous désirez?	what would you like?
vous avez choisi?	have you chosen?
je prends (un café)	I'll have (a coffee)
désolé	I'm very sorry
la personne	person
la femme	woman
le garçon	boy, waiter
le détective	detective

apporter	to bring
regarder	to look at
demander	to ask
il y a	there is/are
il n'y a plus de ...*	there is/are no more ...
je suis	I am
alors	then, well
mon (argent)	my (money)
un autre	another (talking about a masculine noun)
une autre	another (for a feminine noun)

Crime cracker

The detective in this picture is reporting on the movements of the criminal Nicole Lotte, but he is very tired and is making lots of mistakes. Can you write what he should be saying in the space below, changing the things that are wrong?

> **Il est trois heures et quart. Je suis dans le supermarché, en face du café. Il y a seize personnes dans le café. Nicole Lotte est à côté de Rob Debanque. Elle mange des pâtes et il mange un hamburger. Sur la table il y a aussi des lunettes de soleil et deux cuillères. Le garçon apporte un café et un coca.**

Nicole Lotte • Rob Debanque • le détective • les toilettes [f] • la quiche • la carte • l'addition [f] • la crêpe

....
....
....
....
....
....
....

* Here, after **de**, you do not use **le**, **la**, **l'** or **les**. **De** turns into **d'** in front of a word beginning with "a", "e", "i", "o" or "u".

Taking orders

Below you can see what everyone wants to eat and drink. Can you write out each person's order in the red box, using the French for "I'll have a ... and a ..."?

1. ....
....
....
2. ....
....
....
....
3. ....
....
4. ....
....
....
....
5. ....
....
6. ....
....
....

Lunch at the Café Paradis

Can you unjumble this story to find out about Camille's visit to the Café Paradis? Put the numbers of each part of the story in the right order in the green box.

1. **"Il n'y a plus de potage. Nous avons seulement des pizzas et des sandwichs au jambon."**

2. **"Oui. Je voudrais un morceau de quiche et un citron pressé, s'il vous plaît."**

3. **"Oui. Il y a un café en face de la poste. Mais il est fermé."**

4. **"Je prends un potage alors."**

5. **Camille est dans le Café Paradis. Elle regarde la carte.**

6. **"Désolé, il n'y a plus de quiche."**

7. **"Mais je n'aime pas les pizzas, et je suis végétarienne. Il y a un autre café par ici?" demande Camille.**

8. **"Vous avez choisi?" demande le garçon.**

Eating out

Here you will find puzzles which help you practise the French you need when you go out to eat.

Word check

la carte, le menu   menu

Most French restaurants have two kinds of menu, **la carte** and **le menu**. The normal menu is called **la carte**. **Le menu** has set meals which are usually cheaper.

Also good value is **le plat du jour**. This is the dish of the day, or "today's special".

l'entrée [f]	starter
le plat principal	main course
le dessert	dessert, pudding
vous prenez (un dessert)?	are you having (a dessert)?

In France, at mealtimes, it is friendly and polite to say **bon appétit** to people when they are about to start eating. This means "enjoy your meal".

le steak	steak
le poulet	chicken
les champignons [m]	mushrooms
le chou-fleur	cauliflower
les poireaux [m]	leeks
les épinards [m]	spinach
la tarte aux pommes	apple pie, apple tart
la crème caramel*	crème caramel, baked custard
la mousse au chocolat	chocolate mousse
la crème	cream
quel parfum?	which flavour?
la glace à la vanille	vanilla ice-cream
la glace à la fraise	strawberry ice-cream
la glace au chocolat	chocolate ice-cream
la glace au café	coffee ice-cream

Out of order

The waiter in this restaurant has taken five orders without putting the table numbers on them. Decide which one came from which table. Then put the correct number on each order.

un hamburger
un poulet
une salade
des frites
deux cocas

un steak
des frites
une pizza
une salade
une mousse au chocolat
une glace à la fraise

un poulet
un hamburger
une salade
des frites
un coca
un jus d'orange

deux hamburgers
un poulet
une salade
des frites
une glace à la fraise
une crème caramel
une mousse au chocolat

une omelette
une salade
un poulet
des frites
une mousse au chocolat
une glace à la vanille

* This is a favourite French dessert made with eggs, milk and caramel.

24

Supper splash-out

Put the six things on the right into French, and then write them out in the correct spaces (A to F) below, to complete the cartoon story.

A vanilla ice-cream, please.*

Can you pass me the water, please?

One apple pie, please. And one ice-cream.

I haven't got my money!

The bill, please.

One pizza with a salad and one hamburger with some chips, please.

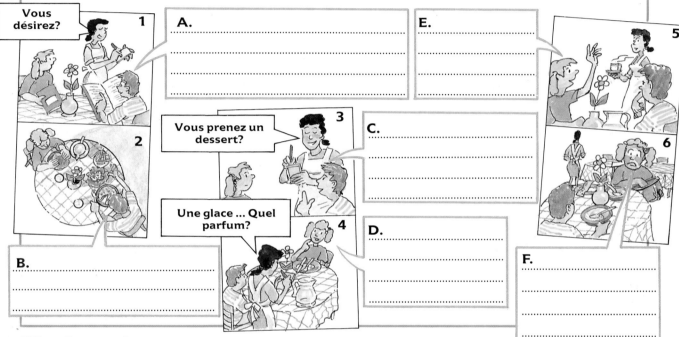

A.

B.

C.

D.

E.

F.

Word search

Can you find French words hidden in this grid and match them with the clues below? Write each one out next to the number of the matching clue, adding its word for "the".

1. The evening meal.
2. The first course.
3. The last course.
4. The place where you eat out.
5. It tells you what you can eat.
6. It tells you what you must pay.
7. He brings you your meal.
8. It might be the main course.
9. A kind of vegetable.
10. Something to drink.
11. You might add this to your dessert.
12. You might drink it after a meal.
13. Something you use for eating desserts.
14. You might add this to your food.

R	S	D	R	A	N	I	P	É	G
F	E	O	S	T	E	A	K	A	C
D	E	S	S	E	R	T	R	D	L
A	Y	C	T	H	L	Ç	A	D	E
C	A	F	É	A	O	C	X	I	N
O	H	T	B	N	U	A	I	T	T
C	U	I	L	L	È	R	E	I	R
A	N	J	S	E	K	T	A	O	É
E	U	C	R	È	M	E	D	N	E
M	B	R	F	D	Î	N	E	R	T

1. ....

2. ....

3. ....

4. ....

5. ....

6. ....

7. ....

8. ....

9. ....

10. ....

11. ....

12. ....

13. ....

14. ....

* Remember, there are two ways of saying "please" in French. Look at the pictures and decide which one you should use for each sentence.

Round-up

These two pages practise lots of the French that you have already used in this book.

French crossword

Use the clues to fill in the crossword. (Don't forget the different words for "a" or "the".)

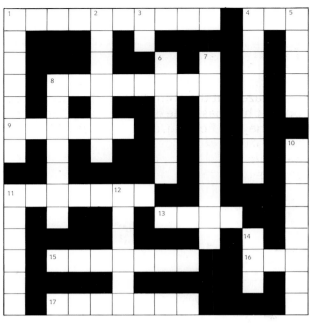

Across

1. What you eat at lunchtime. (2, 8)
4. "The" before more than one thing. (3)
8. Most cars run on this. (1, 7)
9. The end of the day. (2, 4)
11. It is used for measuring. (2, 5)
13. 2 X 4. (4)
15. It is round and grows on a tree. (2, 5)
16. French for "yes". (3)
17. You might toss this in a frying pan. (2, 5)

Down

1. You might sit around this for meals. (2, 5)
2. What you say when you are thirsty. (1, 2, 4)
3. "A" before a masculine noun. (2)
4. You can carry shopping in this. (2, 6)
5. The square of 4. (5)
6. ...**de poires, s'il vous plaît.** (2, 4)
7. Where you can do some shopping. (2, 7)
8. It makes things sweeter. (2, 5)
10. You need this to make bread. (2, 6)
11. It has branches and leaves. (1, 5)
12. You bake things in this. (2, 4)
14. French for "no". (3)

Cracking codes

Can you crack the coded message below to find out where a stolen ring has been hidden? Write the message out properly, and then mark the place where the ring can be found in this picture.

n Eace fe da laverie lutomatique, al i y an uupermarché. sans De lupermarché, sl i y ane uemme fvec an uaddie. clle Eegarde res lruits. fans De laddie, cl i y au doisson, pu dus je domme pt ees darottes. ca Lemme f an uac sn elastique. pa Lague bst eans de lac sn elastique. p

Poison maze

Frédéric has to get through this maze, but the animals will only let him pass if he eats the food they are holding, and some of it is poisonous. If, at each picture junction, he follows the arrow showing what he should say in that picture, Frédéric will avoid any bad food and go the right way. Find his route, then list the safe food he will eat in the red box at the bottom of the page. (Use **le**, **la**, **l'** or **les**.)

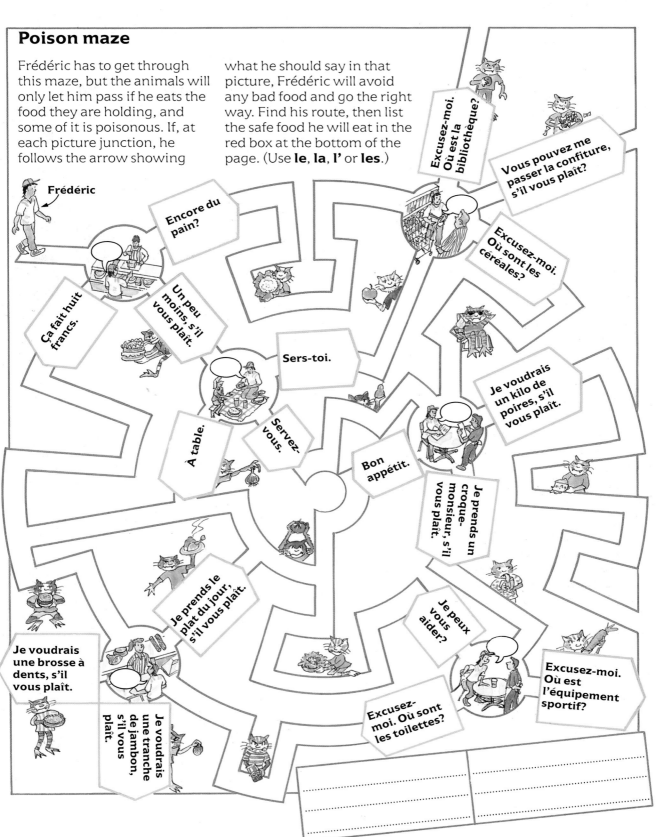

Frédéric

Encore du pain?

Excusez-moi. Où est la bibliothèque?

Vous pouvez me passer la confiture, s'il vous plaît?

Excusez-moi. Où sont les céréales?

Ça fait huit francs.

Un peu moins, s'il vous plaît.

Sers-toi.

Je voudrais un kilo de poires, s'il vous plaît.

À table.

Servez-vous.

Bon appétit.

Je prends un croque-monsieur, s'il vous plaît.

Je prends le plat du jour, s'il vous plaît.

Je peux vous aider?

Je voudrais une brosse à dents, s'il vous plaît.

Je voudrais une tranche de jambon, s'il vous plaît.

Excusez-moi. Où sont les toilettes?

Excusez-moi. Où est l'équipement sportif?

27

Answers to puzzles

p.2-3

Talking nonsense

Jacques: Bonjour, Madame.
Florence: Bonjour, Monsieur.
Frédéric: Au revoir.
Pierre: Pardon.
Yves: Voilà.
Aurélie: Merci.

Word search

The **le** words you can find are:

le bonbon
le livre
le timbre

The **la** words you can find are:

la pomme
la glace
la fleur

The **l'** words you can find are:

l'orange
l'abricot
l'écharpe

In shape

The thing you can see is:

la glace

p.4-5

Shopping in Chèreville

Here you can see Danielle's route:

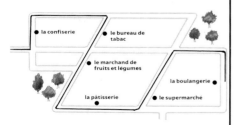

1. Je voudrais un bonbon, s'il vous plaît.*
2. Je voudrais un timbre, s'il vous plaît.
3. Je voudrais une banane, s'il vous plaît.
4. Je voudrais un gâteau, s'il vous plaît.
5. Je voudrais une brosse à dents, s'il vous plaît.
6. Je voudrais un petit pain, s'il vous plaît.

Cartoon confusion

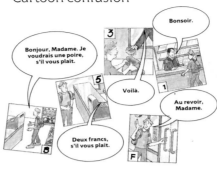

Word chain

1. la glace
2. le biscuit
3. la pêche
4. la poire
5. la banane
6. la casquette
7. l'écharpe
8. le timbre
9. la boucherie
10. le livre
11. la cassette
12. le croissant

p.6-7

Market mix-up

The letters that should go in the speech bubbles are:

1. A   2. C   3. B
4. C   5. B   6. A
7. B

Big spenders

A. Elle a une casquette.
B. Tu as une glace.
C. J'ai huit fleurs.
D. Nous avons dix-huit bonbons.
E. Vous avez sept pommes.

Clued-up

You should have circled sum D.

p.8-9

Torn in two

1. Un kilo de pommes, s'il vous plaît.
2. Ça fait vingt francs.
3. Encore un peu, s'il vous plaît.
4. Oui, s'il vous plaît. Et un morceau de ce fromage.
5. Où sont les vêtements, s'il vous plaît?
6. Où est l'équipement sportif, s'il vous plaît?

Twin shoppers

Elle a un tee-shirt.
Elle a du fromage OR Elle a un morceau de fromage.
Elle a un crayon.
Il a une écharpe.
Il a des biscuits OR Il a un paquet de biscuits.
Il a une bande dessinée.

Shopping search

Je voudrais du pain.
Je voudrais un livre.
Je voudrais des chips.
Je voudrais une glace OR Je voudrais de la glace.
Je voudrais une cassette.
Je voudrais des poires OR Je voudrais une poire.
Je voudrais du jambon.
Je voudrais des biscuits OR Je voudrais un biscuit.
Je voudrais un tee-shirt.

* You can leave **s'il vous plaît** (please) out of your answers, but to be polite, it is best to add it.

p.10-11

Bargain hunter

The hypermarket Pierre should go to is: Prix Cassés.
He will spend: Quatre-vingt-treize francs.
He will save: Quatre francs quatre-vingts.

Treasure trail

A. À côté de la bibliothèque.
B. Devant le marchand de fromages OR Devant le marché.
C. Devant la boulangerie.
D. En face de l'agence de voyages.
E. Devant la pharmacie.

The eighth thing on the list is: une écharpe

The shops on Rue Noire

A. le bureau de tabac
B. le magasin de photo
C. la papeterie
D. le magasin de musique
E. l'office du tourisme
F. le traiteur

p.12-13

Going dotty

Here you can see the maze and, in grey, the route Claudine must take through it to find her dog:

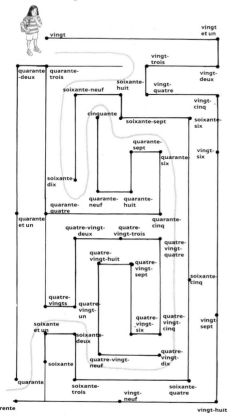

Picture matchmaking

Postcard palaver

1. Excusez-moi. Où est **la poste** (**s'il vous plaît**)?
2. Je voudrais **un timbre**, s'il vous plaît.
3. Pour **l'Angleterre**?
4. **Oui**, s'il vous plaît.
5. C'est **deux francs vingt**.
6. J'ai seulement **un franc**.
7. Il y a **une banque** par ici?
8. Oui. À **droite**, à côté **de la librairie**.
9. Merci. **Au revoir** (**Madame**).
10. Où est **le bureau de change** (**s'il vous plaît**)?
11. Je voudrais **changer un traveller's chèque**, s'il vous plaît.
12. **Fermé**.

p.14-15

Clocking on

1. Le magasin de musique est ouvert de neuf heures vingt à onze heures et demie, et de deux heures moins le quart à sept heures moins le quart.
2. La poste est ouverte de huit heures et quart à midi moins le quart, et de deux heures et quart à cinq heures et quart.
3. La papeterie est ouverte de neuf heures à midi, et de deux heures moins vingt à six heures.
4. La bibliothèque est ouverte de dix heures à une heure dix, et de trois heures à huit heures.

Word circle

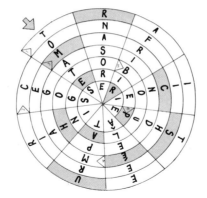

The shop name you can spell is:

le supermarché

Out of time

A. Il est quatre heures vingt-cinq.
B. Il est quatre heures et quart.
C. Il est quatre heures.
D. Il est trois heures et demie.
E. Il est quatre heures dix.

p.16-17

Which way?

1. les saucisses
2. les tomates
3. le chocolat
4. le pique-nique
5. les beignets
6. le jus d'orange
7. les chips
8. les oignons

Triple treat

1. Ils aiment les bananes et les glaces OR Ils aiment les bananes et la glace.
2. Elle aime les oranges et les biscuits.
3. Il aime les oranges et le jambon.
4. Il aime les bananes et les pommes.
5. Elles aiment les fraises et les bonbons.

Food sails

LES BOISSONS:	LA VIANDE:
le café	le pâté
le jus d'orange	le jambon
le thé	la saucisse
l'eau	

LES LÉGUMES:	LES FRUITS:
les petits-pois	la poire
l'oignon	la banane
la carotte	la pomme
la pomme de terre	l'abricot
	la pêche
	l'orange

p.18-19

Sentence splitters

1. Vous aimez les spaghetti mais vous n'aimez pas les frites.
2. Ils aiment le lait mais ils n'aiment pas le jus d'orange.
3. Tu aimes le potage mais tu préfères la pizza.
4. Nous n'aimons pas les oeufs mais nous aimons le yaourt.

French crossword

The perfect picnic

A. Nathalie B. Pierre C. Claudine
Céline Flavien Marc

1. Nathalie et Flavien aiment les biscuits.
2. Marc et Claudine aiment les bananes.
3. Marc et Céline n'aiment pas le café.
4. Nathalie et Céline n'aiment pas les tomates.

p.20-21

Hungry campers

A. Servez-vous.
B. Tu peux me passer la confiture, s'il te plaît?
C. Je peux t'aider?
D. C'est bon?
E. C'est délicieux.
F. Encore du pain?
G. Non, merci. J'ai assez mangé.

Kitchen caper

Le beurre est dans le four.
Les cuillères sont dans le frigo.
Les assiettes sont sous la table.
Le jus d'orange est sur la chaise.
Le gâteau est dans l'évier.
Les fourchettes sont dans la poêle.
Les verres sont sur la table.
Le sel est sur le frigo.

Word snake

1. du fromage
2. du sel
3. du beurre
4. des oeufs
5. du lait
6. une poêle

The word that fits the red grid is:

une omelette

p.22-23

Crime cracker

Il est quatre heures et demie. Je suis dans la cabine téléphonique, en face du café OR Je suis dans une cabine téléphonique, en face du café. Il y a quinze personnes dans le café. Nicole Lotte est en face de Rob Debanque. Elle mange une salade et il mange une pizza. Sur la table il y a aussi une lettre et deux fourchettes. Le garçon apporte un jus d'orange et un thé au citron.

Taking orders

1. Je prends une omelette et un chocolat (chaud).
2. Je prends un morceau de quiche et un (verre de) jus d'orange OR Je prends une quiche et un (verre de) jus d'orange.
3. Je prends un hamburger et un (verre de) coca.
4. Je prends une salade et un (verre de) jus d'orange.
5. Je prends une pizza et un (verre de) coca.
6. Je prends une crêpe et un café.

Lunch at the Café Paradis

The numbers in the right order are:

5, 8, 2, 6, 4, 1, 7, 3.

p.24-25

Out of order

Supper splash-out

A. Une pizza avec une salade et un hamburger avec des frites, s'il vous plaît.
B. Tu peux me passer l'eau, s'il te plaît?
C. Une tarte aux pommes, s'il vous plaît. Et une glace.
D. Une glace à la vanille, s'il vous plaît.
E. L'addition, s'il vous plaît.
F. Je n'ai pas mon argent!

Word search

1. le dîner
2. l'entrée
3. le dessert
4. le restaurant
5. la carte
6. l'addition
7. le garçon
8. le steak
9. les épinards
10. le coca
11. la crème
12. le café
13. la cuillère
14. le sel

p.26-27

French crossword

Cracking codes

En face de la laverie automatique, il y a un supermarché. Dans le supermarché, il y a une femme avec un caddie. Elle regarde les fruits. Dans le caddie, il y a du poisson, du jus de pomme et des carottes. La femme a un sac en plastique. La bague est dans le sac en plastique.

Here you can see where the stolen ring has been hidden:

Poison maze

This is the safe food Frédéric will eat:

le gâteau   la banane
la pomme   le chocolat
la glace   la fraise

French-English word list

Here you can find the French words used in this book with their English meanings. The [m] and [f] after a noun (word for a thing) shows whether it is masculine or feminine.

Most nouns add an "s" when they turn into **les** words (**l'arbre** - tree, **les arbres** - trees). Some work differently, and useful ones are shown here with their **les** words in brackets.

French sometimes has slightly different words for describing things or people, depending on whether they are masculine or feminine. Here, the French you use for a masculine has [m] after it, and the French you use for a feminine has [f].

à	at
l'abricot [m]	apricot
à côté de	next to
l'addition [f]	bill
à droite	on the right
à gauche	on the left
l'agence de voyages [f]	travel agent's
aimer	to like
alors	then, well
l'Angleterre [f]	England
apporter	to bring
l'arbre [m]	tree
l'argent [m]	money
l'assiette [f]	plate
à table	come to the table, the meal is ready
au bout de	at the end of
au citron	with lemon
au lait	with milk
au revoir	goodbye
aussi	also, as well
l'autocollant [m]	sticker
avec	with
avoir	to have (got)
la bague	ring
la baguette	French stick
le ballon	ball
la banane	banana
la bande dessinée	comic (magazine)
la banque	bank
le beignet	doughnut
le beurre	butter
la bibliothèque	library
le biscuit	biscuit
les boissons [f]	drinks
bon appétit	enjoy your meal
le bonbon	sweet
bonjour	hello, good morning/afternoon
bonsoir	good evening
la boucherie	butcher's
la boulangerie	baker's
la brosse à dents	toothbrush
le bureau de change	foreign exchange desk/office

le bureau de tabac	tobacconist
la cabine téléphonique	phone booth
le caddie	trolley
ça fait	that comes to
ça fait combien?	how much does that come to?
le café	café, coffee
le (café) crème	white coffee
le cahier	exercise book
la carotte	carrot
la carte	menu
la carte postale (les cartes postales)	postcard
la casquette	cap
la casserole	saucepan
la cassette	cassette
ce	this
cent grammes de	a hundred grammes of
le centime	centime (French money)
les céréales [f]	cereals
c'est	it/that is
c'est bon?	is it good?
c'est combien?	how much is it/that?
c'est délicieux	it's delicious
c'est tout?	is that all?
la chaise	chair
les champignons [m]	mushrooms
changer	to change, to cash
la charcuterie	delicatessen
les chips [f]	crisps
le chocolat	chocolate
le chocolat (chaud)	hot chocolate
le citron pressé	lemon drink
le coca	coke
comme ça?	like that?
la confiserie	sweet shop
la confiture	jam
le couteau (les couteaux)	knife
le crayon	pencil
la crème	cream
la crème caramel	crème caramel, baked custard
la crêpe	pancake
le croissant	croissant
le croque-monsieur	cheese and ham on toast
la cuillère	spoon
la cuisine	kitchen
dans	in
de ... à	from ... until
le déjeuner	lunch
demander	to ask
derrière	behind
désolé [m], **désolée** [f]	I'm very sorry
le dessert	dessert, pudding
le détective	detective
devant	in front of

le dîner	dinner (evening meal)
du/de la/de l'/des	some
l'eau [f]	water
l'écharpe [f]	scarf
elle	she, it
elles	they
encore du/de la/de l'/des...?	some more...?
encore un peu	a little more
en face de	opposite
entre	between
l'entrée [f]	entrance
l'entrée [f]	starter
les épinards [m]	spinach
l'équipement sportif [m]	sports gear
l'essence [f]	petrol
est	is
et	and
et demie	half past
et quart	quarter past
l'évier [m]	sink
excusez-moi	excuse me
faire la vaisselle	to do the washing up
la farine	flour
la femme	woman
fermé [m], **fermée** [f]	closed
la fleur	flower
le four	oven
la fourchette	fork
la fraise	strawberry
le franc	franc (French money)
le frigo	fridge
les frites [f]	chips
le fromage	cheese
les fruits [m]	fruit
le garçon	boy, waiter
le gâteau (les gâteaux)	cake
la glace	ice-cream
la glace à la fraise	strawberry ice-cream
la glace à la vanille	vanilla ice-cream
la glace au café	coffee ice-cream
la glace au chocolat	chocolate ice-cream
le gobelet	cup, beaker
le hamburger	hamburger
l'hypermarché [m]	hypermarket
il	he, it
il est ... heure(s)	it is ... o'clock
il n'y a plus de/d'	there is/are no more
ils	they
il y a	there is/are
il y a un/une ... par ici?	is there a ... near here?
j'ai assez mangé	I've had enough (to eat)

j'ai faim	I'm hungry
j'ai soif	I'm thirsty
le jambon	ham
je n'aime pas	I don't like
je peux t'aider?	can I help you?
je peux vous aider?	can I help you?
je prends (un café)	I'll have (a coffee)
je suis	I am
je suis végétarien [m], je suis végétarienne [f]	I am a vegetarian
je voudrais...	I would like...
le jus de pomme	apple juice
le jus d'orange	orange juice
là-bas	over there
le lait	milk
la laverie automatique	launderette
le/la/l'/les	the
les légumes [m]	vegetables
la lessive	washing powder
la lettre	letter
la librairie	bookshop
le libre-service	supermarket
le livre	book
les lunettes de soleil [f]	sunglasses
Madame	Mrs.
le magasin	shop, store
le magasin de musique	music shop
le magasin de photo	camera shop
le magasin de sport	sports shop
le magasin de vêtements	clothes shop
mais	but
manger	to eat
le marchand de fromages	cheese stall
le marchand de fruits et légumes	fruit and vegetable shop/stall
le marché	market
le matin	(in the) morning
le menu	set menu
merci	thank you
midi	midday, twelve o'clock
moins le quart	quarter to
mon	my
Monsieur	Mr.
la mousse au chocolat	chocolate mousse
ne ... pas/n' ... pas	not
non	no
l'oeuf [m]	egg
l'office du tourisme [m]	tourist office
l'oignon [m]	onion
l'omelette [f]	omelette
l'orange [f]	orange
ou	or
où est/sont?	where is/are?
oui	yes
ouvert [m], ouverte [f]	open

le pain	bread
le panier	basket
la papeterie	stationer's
pardon	sorry
le passeport	passport
le pâté	pâté
les pâtes [f]	pasta
la pâtisserie	cake shop
la pêche	peach
la pellicule	(camera) film
la personne	person
le petit déjeuner	breakfast
le petit pain	bread roll
les petits-pois [m]	peas
la pharmacie	chemist's, pharmacy
pièce	each
le pique-nique	picnic
la pizza	pizza
le plat du jour (les plats du jour)	dish of the day, "today's special"
le plat principal (les plats principaux)	main course
le plein	a full tank (of petrol)
la poêle	frying pan
la poire	pear
les poireaux [m]	leeks
le poisson	fish
la pomme	apple
la pomme de terre (les pommes de terre)	potato
la poste	post office
le potage	soup
le poulet	chicken
pour	for, to
préférer	to prefer
près de	near
quelle heure est-il?	what time is it?
quel parfum?	which flavour?
la quiche	quiche
regarder	to look at
la règle	ruler
le restaurant	restaurant
la rue	street
le sac en plastique	plastic bag
la salade	salad
la salle à manger	dining room
le sandwich (au fromage/jambon)	(cheese/ham) sandwich
la saucisse	sausage
le sel	salt
sers-toi	help yourself
servez-vous	help yourself, help yourselves
seulement	only
s'il te plaît, s'il vous plaît	please
le soir	(in the) evening
sont	are
la sortie	exit
sous	under
les spaghetti [m]	spaghetti
la station-service	petrol station
le steak	steak

le sucre	sugar
le supermarché	supermarket
sur	on
la table	table
la tarte aux pommes	apple pie, apple tart
le tee-shirt	T-shirt
le thé	tea
le timbre	stamp
les toilettes [f]	toilet
la tomate	tomato
tout	all, everything
le traiteur	delicatessen
le traveller's chèque	traveller's cheque
la trousse	pencil case
tu	you
tu as?	do you have?
tu peux me passer (le beurre)?	can you pass me (the butter)?
un/une	a, an, one
un autre [m], une autre [f]	another
un kilo de	a kilo of
un morceau de/d'	a piece of
un paquet de/d'	a packet of
un peu moins	a little less
une tranche de/d'	a slice of
un verre de/d'	a glass of
vérifier l'huile	to check the oil
le verre	glass
les vêtements [m]	clothes
la viande	meat
voilà	there you are, there you go
votre	your
vous	you
vous avez?	do you have?
vous avez choisi?	have you chosen?
vous désirez?	what would you like?
vous pouvez?	can you?
vous pouvez me passer...?	can you pass me...?
vous prenez (un dessert)?	are you having a (dessert)?
le yaourt	yoghurt

First published in 1993 by Usborne Publishing Ltd, 83-85 Saffron Hill, London EC1N 8RT, England.

Printed in Portugal.